BLOCKCHAIN

Complete Guide To Understanding The Blockchain Technology Revolution And The Future Of Money

MATT COHEN

Copyright © 2017 Matt Cohen - All rights reserved.

In no way is it legal to reproduce, duplicate, or transmit any part of this document in either electronic means or in printed format. recording of this publication is strictly prohibited and any storage of this document is not allowed unless with written permission from the publisher. all rights reserved. The information provided herein is stated to be truthful and consistent, in that any liability, in terms of inattention or otherwise, by any usage or abuse of any policies, processes, or directions contained within is the solitary and utter responsibility of the recipient reader. under no circumstances will any legal responsibility or blame be held against the publisher for any reparation, damages, or monetary loss due to the information herein, either directly or indirectly. Respective authors own all copyrights not held by the publisher. The information herein is offered for informational purposes solely, and is universal as so. the presentation of the information is without contract or any type of guarantee assurance. The trademarks that are used are without any consent, and the publication of the trademark is without permission or backing by the trademark owner. all trademarks and brands within this book are for clarifying purposes only and are the owned by the owners themselves, not affiliated with this document. The author wishes to thank the following people for the images of this book: Theymos, Samueldrozdov, coinbase.com, Gareth Halfacree, Youwei-han, bitcoincharts.com. Unless specified differently, all the images are released under Creative Commons CC-BY-SA License.

BLOCKCHAIN

MATT COHEN

TABLE OF CONTENTS

Free Bonus: Make Money Online - 5 Proven And Legitimate Ways To Earn Money From Your Computer	7
Introduction	9
Chapter 1: Understanding the Blockchain Technology	11
What is blockchain?	11
Brief history of blockchain technology	12
How does blockchain work?	12
Understanding the blockchain database	13
What is a distributed ledger?	14
The concept behind the 51% attack	14
Smart contract	15
Advantages and disadvantages of using blockchain	16
Is there a private blockchain?	20
Other uses of blockchain technology	22
Chapter 2: Blockchain and Cryptocurrencies	27
What are cryptocurrencies?	27
Who uses cryptocurrencies?	28
Who is Satoshi Nakamoto?	30
How cryptocurrencies apply the blockchain technology	30
Kinds of cryptocurrency wallets	31

How to keep your cryptocurrency wallet safe and secure	35
How a transaction works and appears on the blockchain	37
Beware of the fork	37
On legal matters	40
Other kinds of cryptocurrencies	41
Chapter 3: Ways to Profit	**47**
Make money	47
Investing	47
Trading	48
Mining	48
Gambling	52
Make your own cryptocurrency	53
Strategies	55
Common mistakes	62
Chapter 4: The Future of Blockchain	**67**
Possible future developments	67
How blockchain can affect financial services and other employment	70
The future of money	72
Now and then	73
Conclusion	**75**
Other Books By Matt Cohen	**77**

MATT COHEN

FREE BONUS
MAKE MONEY ONLINE - 5 PROVEN AND LEGITIMATE WAYS TO EARN MONEY FROM YOUR COMPUTER

The majority of people thinks earning an income through the internet is just a dream, or alternatively some sort of scam. However, there are many legitimate ways to earn money from your computer.

In this short guide you're about to discover 5 proven ways you can follow to actually start making money online, for real. Each one comes with a rating based on 3 factors:

- How quick can you actually earn your first dollar? (5 stars = really quick)
- Is it easy for a beginner with little to no previous experience? (5 stars = really easy)
- Is it cheap to start or does it require a high investment? (5 stars = really cheap or free)

Go to **www.eepurl.com/c5Ybb1** to download the free guide.

MATT COHEN

INTRODUCTION

Congratulations on downloading this book and thank you for doing so.

The following chapters will teach you everything that you need to know about the blockchain technology, as well as its practical applications.

Chapter 1 discusses the basics of the blockchain technology. Before you know how blockchain is used in cryptocurrency, as well as its other applications, you should first have a good understanding of how the blockchain technology works.

Chapter 2 focuses more on cryptocurrencies. Although blockchain has many uses, it is often associated with cryptocurrencies like Bitcoin, for good reason. This chapter will give you a good foundation on cryptocurrencies and how blockchain technology is used to power such cryptocurrencies.

Chapter 3 teaches you how you can earn a profit by investing in cryptocurrency. Learn about the different strategies that you can use to significantly turn the odds in your favor.

Chapter 4 talks about the future of the blockchain technology. Find out where this exciting technology is headed, and understand why learning and investing in blockchain today might just be the best decision that you can make.

There are plenty of books on this subject on the market, thanks again for choosing this one! Every effort was made to ensure it is full of as much useful information as possible. Please enjoy!

CHAPTER 1
UNDERSTANDING THE BLOCKCHAIN TECHNOLOGY

What is blockchain?

Simply put, the blockchain technology is a form of a distributed ledger that is decentralized and public. It records transactions and has a very high level of security.

The blockchain, or which was originally called as *block chain* (two words), is a list of records referred to as *blocks*. These blocks are linked together and secured by cryptography. Cryptography is the practice of securing communication. It deals with confidentiality and security of information.

Every block in the chain is linked to a previous block with a hash pointer. There is also a time stamp and transaction data. The blockchain ensures the integrity of every block or record by recording the transactions across a network of computers. This way, no record can be altered or modified without changing the other blocks. Being a public ledger, all users can verify and audit any and all of the transactions. Since the blockchain technology is decentralized, it is free from control or influence of any central authority. Even the founder or developer of a blockchain cannot change the records without the consent of or notice to all the other users.

Brief history of blockchain technology

When talking about the history of blockchain technology, most people would think that it was first developed by Satoshi Nakamoto. However, it is worth noting that the first work on creating secured chain of blocks using cryptography was made back in the year 1991 by W. Scott Stornetta and Stuart Haber. However, the work was considered incomplete and lacking some material elements. It was only when Satoshi Nakamoto entered the picture in 2008 and conceptualized a blockchain that powered the cryptocurrency known as Bitcoin the following year. The work of Satoshi Nakamoto is the first distributed blockchain in the world. Hence, most people regard Satoshi Nakamoto as the developer or even the founder of blockchain technology.

How does blockchain work?

Here is an illustration of how a transaction works on a blockchain: X wants to send some money to Z. This transaction will be represented as a *block*. Now, this block will be broadcast to all the parties in the network. All those in the network will approve the said transaction as valid. After confirmation, the said block will be added to the chain, and the money is then transferred from X to Z.

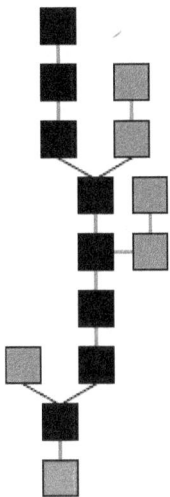

Blockchain formation: the darker blocksrepresent the main chain. Orphan blocks exist outside of the main chain.

It is worth noting that that the blockchain technology is being revolutionary not just because it is used to power cryptocurrency transactions, rather, it is because it can be applied to cover every form of transaction that involves value. Hence, it is not just limited to cryptocurrency or money, but can also cover goods and property.

Understanding the blockchain database

There are two things that you will find when you look at a blockchain database: blocks and transactions. What is a block? A block is a valid transaction hashed and encoded on the blockchain. In order to connect it to the previous block, every new block contains the hash of the block before it.

Here is a simple example: Let us say that person A sends some bitcoins to person B. The wallet address of person A will appear on the blockchain with a corresponding cryptocurrency amount that it is sending to B. Of course, neither A nor B will be named on the network, but only their wallet addresses will appear as well as the amount involved in the transaction. The blockchain will show and keep a record of the transaction, including a time stamp. It will also show the transactions that have already been confirmed, as well as those that are yet to be confirmed.

When you refer to a link of blocks, you call it as a *chain*. As you can see, the blockchain technology is not really hard to understand. The process of every block being linked to the previous block continues up to the *genesis block*. The genesis block is the very first block in a blockchain.

What is a distributed ledger?

So, what exactly does a distributed ledger do? The concept of a distributed ledger means that any changes to the ledger shall be shared with and synchronized across the entire network. For example, if X makes a change to the ledger, the said alteration will automatically appear on Y's ledger, if they belong to the same blockchain. Other users of the blockchain will see the said change. Take note that the users in a blockchain do not view separate ledgers from one another. Rather, the whole blockchain network uses a single ledger, and all changes are made and spread across the network instantly in real time.

The concept behind the 51% attack

The 51% attack refers to the security of the blockchain technology. What it means is that for an attack against the blockchain to be successful, it must have at least 51% of the total hash rate of the blockchain network that is being attacked or hacked. Take note that the blockchain network is composed of a wide network of computers, which gives it a very high hash rate. This makes it virtually invincible from any attack.

It is worth noting that the 51% concept does not mean that a blockchain cannot be attacked. An attack against a blockchain with less than 51% hash rate is still possible. However, such attack may have no chance of being successful. Also, an attack with more than 51% hash rate does not guarantee the success of the said attack.

Smart contract

A smart contract is a code that is present in a network of blocks. It defines conditions, and when these conditions are met, all the computers in a network shall execute the contract. This assures the users to get the intended outcome. Smart contracts can be applied to blockchain technology. At present, the most famous cryptocurrency that uses smart contracts is the cryptocurrency known as Ethereum. Ethereum is one of the most successful cryptocurrencies in the market today. At present, it is the next in rank after bitcoin.

Here is an example to illustrate how smart contracts work: Let us say that the shipper, W, has to deliver a particular item to person Z. Although Z trusts W, he does not trust X, the person assigned to deliver the item. Hence, Z will enter into an agreement with W to just pay for the item after delivery. This is to ensure compliance, especially in this case where Z does not trust the person who will deliver the item. However, this approach is quite complicated and normally involves third parties. Also, a problem may arise if W would like to assure that he will be paid and does not agree with the terms offered by Z.

With the use of smart contracts, this can be simplified. Instead of sending your payment to W, Z simply has to pay the shipment to a smart contract on the day of loading. The smart contract will then hold the said payment until Z confirms the delivery of the item. After delivery and upon confirmation, the money paid by Z will then be immediately released to W.

Smart contracts do not just set the conditions, they also can execute the terms of the contracts. This makes them very versatile. Although it is true that, for now, a smart contract can only handle simple terms or tasks, just imagine how much complicated terms it can handle and execute if you set up a high number of smart contracts.

Advantages and disadvantages of using blockchain

Just like any other technology, the blockchain technology also has its advantages and disadvantages. Let us examine them one by one:

- Advantages

High integrity

Users can be confident that the process will be executed in accordance with the protocol. They do not have to worry about any intervention that a third party might make. Once a transaction is confirmed, there is literally no way to cancel, withdraw, or modify it.

Trustless

No, this does not mean that you cannot trust it. Rather, what this means is that no trust is required for the execution of any transaction. The reason is that there is no intermediary involved. Hence, there is no third party who can get in the way of the transaction. Provided that the specific conditions are met, you can rest assured that the smart contracts will execute the agreement automatically. Hence, it is also an effective way to remove counterparty risk.

Trusted data

You can rest assured that the data transmitted by the blockchain is trusted and reliable. Moreover, the data will always be complete, accurate, and timely. Since a blockchain is a public ledger, the information that you may need is also widely available.

Fair transparency

The blockchain technology is a public ledger. As such, any data or information is viewable to the public. This creates transparency and fairness.
More simplified version
Instead of having to look at different ledgers, all the transactions made over the blockchain are added to a single ledger. Hence, you will not have to worry about monitoring and analyzing different ledgers at the same time.

Round the clock availability

The blockchain functions on its own without need of any central authority to regulate or look after it. As such, it is available 24/7. What is more, since it exists online, it is not limited to any geographical location. Sending or receiving money/cryptocurrency to a friend located on the other side of the world is as fast as sending to or receiving from someone in the same neighborhood.

Quicker transaction

The blockchain technology operates much faster than traditional banks. You can send and receive money or cryptocurrency almost instantly. Unlike dealing with traditional banks or other third-party financial services, there is no need for you to wait for clearing and final settlement when you use blockchain. Everything happens online and they happen almost instantly with just a few clicks of a mouse.

Cheaper transaction fee

Since the blockchain technology eliminates the use of a middleman, you can save more money in terms of the transaction fee. This is helpful, especially if you intend to send or receive money on a regular basis. In the long run, the amount that you can save from the lower transaction fee can pile up into a significant amount.

- Disadvantages

Unregulated

Cryptocurrencies are well known for being unregulated. In fact, such unregulated status is often considered a strength. However, it also poses some risks. Due to its unregulated status, many people are cautious of using it. They think that since it is regulated and every blockchain has its own developers, then the blockchain is susceptible to being manipulated. However, as you already know by now, such manipulation is impossible. Unfortunately, many people do not bother to understand how the blockchain really works. The good news is that the blockchain technology is getting more popular these days, and more people are getting interested in learning how it works. Once they understand why an unregulated blockchain is more secured than a regulated one, then they will be happy to trust and use this new technology.

New technology

Although the blockchain is hitting the world like storm, it is still a fairly new technology. It is much less than perfect, and there are still many rooms for development — which is a good thing. However, this technology aims to cover so many aspects, such a speed of transaction, verification process, limitation on data, and others. These things are important to the entire process of the blockchain network. Unfortunately, considering that it is still a new technology still in its developing stage, there is a risk that it may fail to sustain itself in the long run.

High start-up cost

It is true that using blockchain technology will allow you to cut down your expenses. However, switching to blockchain and setting up the system may cost you some money. Hence, even though it will save you some money in the long run, be ready to spend money for a start.

Increasing energy requirement

The more the network expands, the more energy it will need. Here is an example: The cryptocurrency, bitcoin, uses 450 thousand and trillion solutions every second simply to validate transactions. This energy consumption continues to increase as bitcoin's network continues to broaden. So, just imagine how much more energy the network will have to consume a few years from now.

Security risk

It is true that the blockchain technology prides itself with high security that makes it virtually invulnerable to attacks, it does not mean that there is 100% guarantee that it is totally risk-free. After all, many hackers out there also develop their knowledge and skills. Another security issue is that since the blocks are linked to one another, a single bug that penetrates the system can pose a serious threat to the entire network.

Lack of trust

Unfortunately, even though one of the strengths of a blockchain technology is its high security and integrity, many people still do not trust its system. The problem here is not really the lack of trust, but lack of understanding. Many people do not keep an open mind and do not want to bother to learn just how the blockchain technology works. Instead of studying it, they simply dismiss the idea immediately and stick to the traditional practice.

Is there a private blockchain?

When people talk about blockchain, they often associate it with bitcoin. It is worth noting that bitcoin's blockchain is a public blockchain, which means that it is open to everyone. Now, you might wonder, if there is a public blockchain, would it also be possible to have a private blockchain? It is true that when people define what a blockchain is, they always say that it is of a public nature. However, it is worth noting that a blockchain can also be private.

In the case of a private blockchain, there is an organization that controls the network and has the authority to encode data on the blockchain. Hence, it is important that the said organization should be trusted by the users since it can alter and modify the blocks, and even add or remove blocks as it pleases. In fact, it has the power to control users from reading any data, which also means that it can prevent users from doing so. When it comes to auditing the transactions, unlike a public blockchain where everyone can verify the transactions, a private blockchain enjoys greater privacy. Also, unlike a public blockchain where a transaction can no longer be cancelled or changed once confirmed, a private blockchain can still make changes even after confirmation of a transaction through its regulating organization.

An advantage of using a private blockchain is that it can enjoy quicker transactions with less fees since even a small number of computers or devices would be enough to verify transactions. Also, since a private blockchain would have a smaller scope than a public one, it can easily be fixed. Also, since the users trust the organization that exercises authority over the network, human intervention can be relied on in case of problems, which can allow for a quick and easy fix. However, unlike a public blockchain, a private blockchain is vulnerable to being manipulated by the organization that exercises authority over it.

Is it still worth it to use a private blockchain? Given

the choice, a public blockchain is so much better, especially if you will have to deal with people that you do not know personally. However, if you just want to use the blockchain for simple tasks, recordings, or verification, and if you will be dealing with people whom you are sure you can trust, then a private blockchain may be sufficient for your need.

Other uses of blockchain technology

It is worth noting that the blockchain being applied to cryptocurrency is just the beginning. Its technology can also be harnessed for other purposes. Here are some examples on how the blockchain technology can be used in business and other purposes:

Smart contract in motorcycle rental

Smart contracts were made popular by Ethereum Project; Ethereum is another type of cryptocurrency. It is defined as a "decentralized platform that runs smart contracts: applications that run exactly as programmed without any possibility of downtime, censorship, fraud or third-party interference." Smart contracts are self-automated programs that have the ability to execute a contract provided certain conditions are met. An excellent example of how this is applied in business is the company known as Slock. It uses an Ethereum-enabled platform that automatically unlocks the locks of motorcycles once an agreement has been made between the parties.

Supply chain management and communication

Blockchain can provide a more effective supply chain. For example, there are businesses that get their materials from multiple suppliers. The problem with this approach is that if a part of the entire process fails, then the finished product may suffer. In turn, this is not good for the business. With blockchain technology, you can view a verifiable record which can show the stare of the product at every stage of the process. An example of a company that takes advantage of this and uses the blockchain technology is SkuChain.

Payment of employees

Applying blockchain in the payment of employees can also be beneficial for both the employers and employees. This is true, especially if you have to compensate employees who are located in other countries on a regular basis. Using a cryptocurrency can be a cost-saver. In fact, there is now a payroll known as Bitwage that will help you do this. Of course, you do not need the service of such site; you can do it on your own once you have a cryptocurrency wallet.

Reliable electronic voting

The blockchain technology has a high security. Since there is no authority that controls it, except in the case of a private blockchain, then you can rest assured that it is free from any form of manipulation. It can also be used in case where you need a tally of votes. For example, in case of stockholder approval in companies. There is now what is called as BitShares which is a distributed database which uses Delegated Proof of State or DPOS. It states that "DPOS leverages the power of stakeholder approval voting to resolve consensus issues in a fair and democratic way. All network parameters, from fee schedules to block intervals and transaction sizes, can be tuned via elected delegates. Deterministic selection of block producers allows transactions to be confirmed in an average of just 1 second. Perhaps most importantly, the consensus protocol is designed to protect all participants against unwanted regulatory interference."

Counterfeit solution

Counterfeiting is one of the common problems in business. It is a problem that modern commerce continuously faces. The current solution is to depend upon a third party between customers and merchants. Now, with blockchain technology, there is no more need for any third-party service just to ensure the authenticity of a product. Imagine a blockchain where merchants and marketplaces are well connected. The transparency and integrity offered by blockchain would be enough that stakeholders will no longer need a third party just to confirm the authenticity of branded products.

As you can see, there are many uses of blockchain technology. Thousands of patents have already been filed that utilize the blockchain technology.

Electricity provider

Instead of the power being sent to the entire neighborhood from a central power, the electricity can be sent via a distributed network patterned after blockchain technology. With the use of solar and roof-top high-powered battery technology, it is possible that individual houses can be used as distributive power providers themselves. According to Goldman Sachs, the blockchain technology can be utilized to "secure transactions of power between individuals on a distributed network who do not have an existing relationship."

MATT COHEN

CHAPTER 2
BLOCKCHAIN AND CRYPTOCURRENCIES

What are cryptocurrencies?

Cryptocurrencies are a form of digital money. They are used as a substitute of money. Take note that cryptocurrencies are not considered as legal tender. They are not controlled by any central authority. Since cryptocurrencies are not considered as legal tender, they cannot be used by a debtor to compel a creditor to accept the payment, except if payment using cryptocurrency is agreed upon in the contract.

Among all the cryptocurrencies out there, Bitcoin is the most popular. It is the leading cryptocurrency trusted by many individuals and merchants worldwide. However, it is worth noting that there are many other cryptocurrencies out there. In fact, there are more than 900 different cryptocurrencies that have already been created. However, only a few are able to last long and remain in circulation in the market.

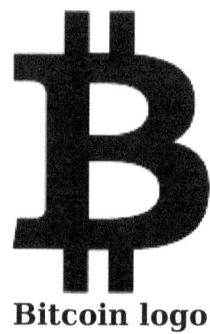
Bitcoin logo

The thing about cryptocurrency is that they do not actually exist. They do not exist in the sense that they have no physical existence. You cannot point your finger at it and say, "That is my bitcoin." When you access your cryptocurrency wallet, you will not see any actual coin on the screen. Rather, what you will see is just a number that shows the total amount of cryptocurrency that you have, as well as a record of transactions, if any.

Who uses cryptocurrencies?

Many individuals and businesses these days use cryptocurrencies. The good news is that more and more people want to learn how to use them. Basically, cryptocurrencies have their own value and are used as a substitute for money. A good example of cryptocurrency user is Microsoft. Yes, that computer giant. Microsoft now accepts bitcoin as a medium of payment. This started way back in 2014. Now, Microsoft users can buy from Microsoft and Xbox stores using bitcoin. It is also worth noting that Microsoft was also behind the Azure Blockchain. Azure Blockchain is a platform that helps large businesses with their financial data. Of course, Microsoft is not the only business that is open to the use of cryptocurrency. Another software giant, Intuit, also accepts bitcoin payments. Now, this may surprise you, but even PayPal now accepts bitcoin. It broadcast its intention to do so as early as September 2014. There are other known businesses that accept and use bitcoins, such as Dish Network, fiverr, and Overstock.com, among others. In fact, it is now possible to book a hotel room or even an air flight and pay for it using cryptocurrency. To date, it appears that most businesses and individuals are more open to the use of bitcoins than any other cryptocurrency. However, it is possible that other cryptocurrencies will soon be as acceptable as bitcoin.

You might be wondering, how come many other businesses have not yet jumped into the cryptocurrency bandwagon? Well, there are two main reasons why: The first reason is volatility. Cryptocurrencies like bitcoin have a high volatility. Their price can fluctuate significantly within a single day. However, this is not always a bad thing. In fact, it is its high volatile nature that makes it a very lucrative investment. Another reason is the possibility of government interference. As long as governments leave it alone, then bitcoin and even other cryptocurrencies will most probably have good developments. However, the problem is that once the government begins to interfere just as what is happening now, then complications may arise, and the stability of cryptocurrencies may be questioned. The legal matters, as well as why the government may regulate the use of cryptocurrencies will be discussed in more detail later in this book.

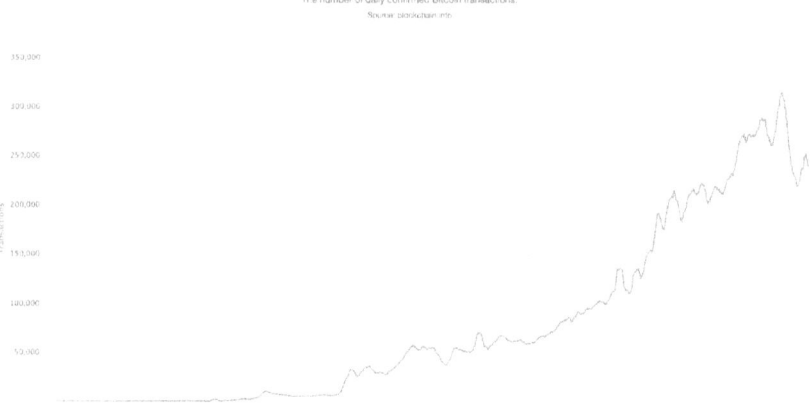

The number of daily confirmed Bitcoin transactions from January 2009 to September 2017

Who is Satoshi Nakamoto?

The truth is that nobody knows the real identity of Satoshi Nakamoto. Some people claim that Satoshi Nakamoto is composed of a group of people, while others say that Satoshi Nakamoto might even be a woman. The name Satoshi Nakamoto appeared as the author of a white paper that was published to a cryptography mailing list on October 31, 2008. The paper was entitled, "Bitcoin: A Peer-to-Peer Electronic Cash System." The following year, the famous cryptocurrency of all, Bitcoin, was finally introduced in the market. Today, Bitcoin is the most famous and successful cryptocurrency. In fact, when it comes to cryptocurrency, Bitcoin has become the leading standard that other cryptocurrencies have been categorized as *altcoin*, which is short for alternative coin. Hence, although nobody knows who Satoshi Nakamoto really is, his legacy, Bitcoin, continues to thrive in the market.

How cryptocurrencies apply the blockchain technology

Cryptocurrencies like Bitcoin use the blockchain technology. Every transaction that occurs gets a corresponding record on the blockchain. For example, if person A sends a bitcoin to person B, a corresponding record will reflect on the blockchain network, which is viewable by the public. Do not worry; only your wallet address will appear. Hence, your personal identity will remain confidential.

Kinds of cryptocurrency wallets

Before you can start sending or receiving any cryptocurrency, you first need to have a cryptocurrency wallet. Obviously, it is just a place where you store your cryptocurrency. It is worth noting that there are different kinds of cryptocurrency wallets. It is important that you understand their differences in order to know the kind of wallet that will best suit your needs.

There are two main classifications of cryptocurrency wallets: hot wallet and cold wallet. So, what is the difference between the two? A hot wallet is a cryptocurrency wallet that exists online, while a cold wallet, also known as cold storage, is stored offline.

On the one hand, a hot wallet is more convenient to use than a cold wallet since you can easily and quickly access it just by going online. However, the drawback is that it offers less security than a cold wallet. On the other hand, a cold wallet, although more secure, is not as convenient to use as a hot wallet since it is stored offline.

Hot and cold wallets are only general classifications. They can be further specified into the following:

Web wallet

A web wallet is also known as an online wallet. A good example of a web wallet is Coinbase. It is like using any other secured site where you input a password to access your account. This is, in fact, the most common cryptocurrency wallet. More than 60% of cryptocurrency users use this type of wallet. Since accessing the Internet using a mobile phone has become common these days, many web wallets can now be accessed via mobile.

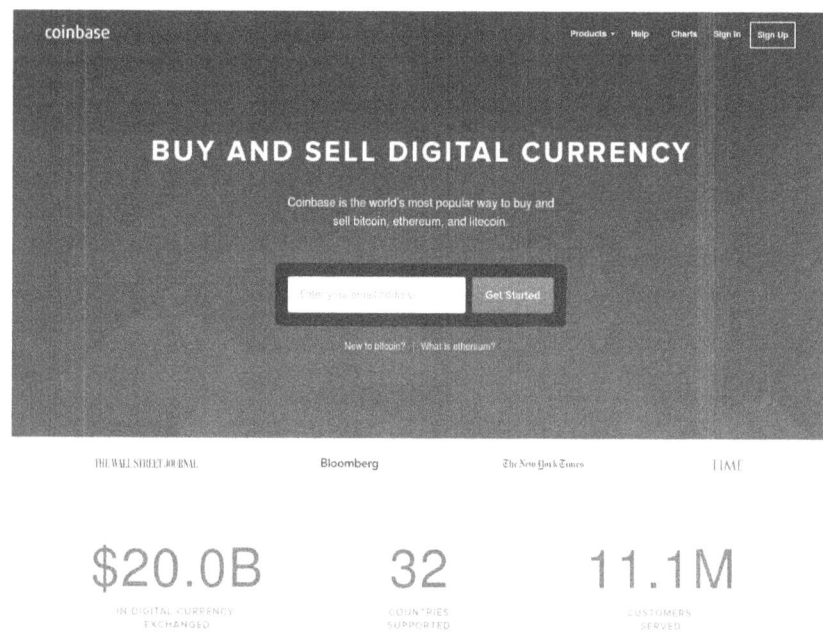

A screenshot of coinbase.com

Mobile wallet

A mobile wallet is a cryptocurrency wallet application that you can download on your mobile phone. Many web wallets also have a mobile feature. A mobile wallet seems to offer the lowest security and has the potential to compromise your privacy since many of these applications require permission to access some information on your mobile phone, such as media files and others. Hence, be sure to read the terms and conditions before you download any mobile wallet. Still, a mobile wallet is very convenient to use. In fact, it may be considered as the most convenient among all the cryptocurrency wallets.

Hardware wallet

A hardware wallet functions as a cold wallet. Hence, although it is less convenient, it offers higher security. When you use a hardware wallet, you keep your cryptocurrency in some hardware such as a USB. This way your cryptocurrency will not be exposed to the Internet. It is worth noting that it is the exposure to the Internet that can compromise the security of your wallet. This is the reason why many people decide to use a cold wallet. Once something is exposed to the Internet, then it can become a target by hackers and scammers. Just be sure not to lose your hardware wallet; otherwise, it will be almost impossible to recover your cryptocurrency.

Ledger HW.1 bitcoin hardware wallet attached to a key ring

Desktop wallet

A desktop wallet is just like a hardware wallet. However, instead of storing your cryptocurrencies in some hardware or USB, you store them in a computer. You do not need to use the latest model. An old desktop or laptop computer will work just fine, as long as it has a well-functioning operating system. Take note that if the said computer has been previously connected to the Internet, it is strongly advised that you reformat the computer before using it for cold storage. Again, when it comes to security, it is best for the cold wallet to be not connected to the Internet. Only connect your cold wallet to the Internet when the need arises. Just like a hardware wallet, be sure that the computer where you will be storing your cryptocurrency is in a safe place where it will not be broken or stolen. This is the drawback when using cold storage. Although there is no risk as much as online threats or attacks are concerned, there is still the risk of losing your cold wallet or the risk of your wallet getting broken.

Paper wallet

A paper wallet is a popular type of cryptocurrency wallet. Take note that unlike other cold wallets, you do not store your cryptocurrency in a paper wallet. Rather, what you will be storing will be your public and private keys. These keys act like a password; they are needed to access your account. A paper wallet can also store a QR code that can be scanned to access your account.

A common practice is to have several copies of your paper wallet, so that you will have extra copies in case you misplace it. Just be sure to keep them in a safe place.

How to keep your cryptocurrency wallet safe and secure

Security is of utmost importance when you use cryptocurrency. Therefore, you should be aware of the best practices that you should observe in order to keep your account safe and secure:

Strong password

Make sure that you use a password that would be impossible to predict. A good way to do this is by combining upper and lower-case letters. You should also use numbers and symbols. Make sure that you do not use a password that people can easily guess with just some trial and error. Hence, avoid using your name or your birthday as a password. It is also advised that you change your password from time to time. However, when you do change your password, make sure that you do it in a secure environment.

Two-factor authentication

Many wallets will allow you to add another layer of protection to your account known as two-factor authentication or simply 2-FA. This feature will generate a password that changes within a short period of time. Normally, you will receive the code on your mobile phone, and you simply have to input it after your password in order to login to your wallet. Many people do not use this feature because they consider it a hassle. However, it is recommended that you enable the 2-FA protection. After all, you will only need it if every time you log in to your account. Once logged in, then you will not be bothered by it anymore. Another good thing about using this feature is that it makes your account virtually impossible to be hacked, since the code changes in a few seconds. To access your account, the hacker must be in possession of your phone.

Site security

Before you input any confidential details such as your wallet password, be sure that the site is secure. Many hackers and scammers use phishing or fake sites to steal sensitive information. Fortunately, it is easy to know if the site is secure. Just beside the page's URL, you should be able to see a green padlock or even read the word "Secure." Make sure that you pay attention to this before you key in your password.

Avoid unsecured connections

Never access your wallet using a public Wi-Fi connection. Regardless whether you are in a restaurant, bar, or at the mall, keep in mind not to access your cryptocurrency wallet if connected to public Wi-Fi's. This is true even if you see that the site or page is secure. The reason is that the very connection that you have to the Internet is not secure enough. There is a good chance that a hacker can be able to view whatever it is that you are typing. So, remember not to access your cryptocurrency wallet when you are connected to a public or any unsecured connection.

Security checks for cold storage

When it comes to cold wallets, make sure that you use something that has a good quality, so that it will not be broken. Also, be sure to keep it in a place where it will be safe and will not be stolen. Never use something that is connected or has been previously connected to the Internet, except if you can reformat it completely. While using it as a cold storage, never expose it to the Internet.

How a transaction works and appears on the blockchain

A cryptocurrency transaction has three main parts, namely: Input, amount, and the recipient's address. The blockchain takes notes of all these things and even records a time stamp of a transaction. To better illustrate the process, here is a simple example: Let us say that X sends 10 bitcoins to H. Before X can send 10 bitcoins, X must first have 10 bitcoins in his cryptocurrency wallet. This part is referred to as the *input*. The amount of bitcoin to be transferred is also taken note of. In this case, it is 10 bitcoins. The next part is the wallet address of the recipient. In this example, it is the wallet address of H that will receive the 10 bitcoins sent by X.

The blockchain will also show once a certain transaction has been confirmed. Do not forget that when you use blockchain technology, every transaction that gets confirmed can no longer be canceled, reversed, or modified.

Beware of the fork

It is not uncommon for cryptocurrencies to experience significant fluctuations in price. Such event, especially if it ends up with a significant drop in price may be called as a *fork*. The best way to understand a fork is to know how it is made:

It is worth noting that all cryptocurrencies use computer generated codes. In fact, these codes are what allow a cryptocurrency to create digital money. Like any other computer program, the codes used by any cryptocurrency can be modified or changed. Now, when making any modifications, it should be made with caution to avoid becoming incompatible with the previous version. Now, it is in the alteration or modification of such codes that may result in a fork.

There are two kinds of forks: an accidental fork and a hard fork. An accidental fork is nothing serious. It is only temporary and has less impact. The developer can easily resolve such issue. An accidental fork usually happens when an update is made, but said update fails to match the previous version due to slight incompatibilities. The result is that a person will end up with two different ledgers instead of just a single ledger: One ledger for the old version, and another ledger for the new one. In this case, the developer simply needs to fix the discrepancy and merge the two ledgers together. Now, a hard fork is like an accidental fork; however, a hard fork has a much stronger impact. In case of a hard fork, there will be more incompatibilities between the previous version and the updated version. Hence, more time and effort will be needed to fix the discrepancy. In addition, the users of the cryptocurrency concerned will have to update all related applications in order to enjoy all the features and properly use the cryptocurrency. Another difference is that a hard fork creates a completely different or new path in the blockchain.

What can you expect when there is a fork? Well, any kind of fork can be stressful to cryptocurrency users. Hence, every fork, accidental or serious, needs to be fixed as quickly as possible. A fork can have the effect of bypassing or delaying transactions, which is not good for businesses that are using the said cryptocurrency under a fork. In such case, they will have to simply wait until the developers fix the issues. Now, it is worth noting that a fork is not always a bad thing, at least not if you change your perspective. Some traders turn it into an opportunity. Normally, when there is a fork, especially a hard fork, it would cause the price of the cryptocurrency concerned to decrease. And, after the fork, its price increases and recovers from the effects of the fork. As you can see, this can be a profitable opportunity. The reason why the price of a cryptocurrency decreases during a fork is that this event tends to cause panic in the cryptocurrency community. Hence, transactions are kept on hold or are let go, and cryptocurrency users may even shift to another cryptocurrency just to avoid the fork. This, of course, can tend to decrease the value of the cryptocurrency that is experiencing a fork. It is worth noting that developers should, as much as possible, be more careful and avoid creating a fork, even an accidental fork. The reason is that the cryptocurrency community may start to lose trust and confidence and completely switch to a competitor. In this case, the cryptocurrency that experienced a fork may no longer be able to recover even after the fork.

Now, forks are nothing new. In fact, they can be considered a normal part of any cryptocurrency. After all, no matter how keen the developers are, it is hard to avoid making a mistake, especially slight mistakes that can lead to an accidental fork. So, if you engage in cryptocurrencies, you can expect to face a few forks along the way. Now, what should you do in case of a fork? The beast way to respond to a fork is to be prepared for it. Remember that in case of a fork, the best thing that you can do is to stay calm. Be objective. Do not be like the others who panic and get stressed out. Since you are already expecting that a fork will happen, then there is no reason for you to panic. Instead, what you should do is to get as much information as you can about the fork, and then make a decision as to how you would respond to it. Are you going to pull out your investments or wait for the fork to settle down? It is also a good advice to pay attention to how other cryptocurrency users react to it. Online cryptocurrency forums and groups would be helpful for this purpose. Also try to find out how long it would take for the developers to fix the fork. It is also common for developers to post a message regarding the fork, as well as the steps that they are doing to resolve it. Just keep in mind that forks are nothing extraordinary. In fact, many cryptocurrency users are getting used to it already. So, just stay calm, think objectively, and come up with the best course of action.

On legal matters

Since cryptocurrency users enjoy so much anonymity and other benefits, it is not hard to understand why the government takes interest on this matter. Now, it is clear that cryptocurrencies are not controlled or regulated by any central authority or government. However, this does not mean that a state, through its government and instrumentalities, cannot regulate its use within its territorial jurisdiction.

At present, many states are starting to regulate its use, such as applying KYC Policy (Know Your Customer Policy), and others. Since governments cannot regulate the cryptocurrency itself, they tend to regulate the online service provider and the banks regarding cryptocurrency deposits and withdrawals. In other states such as Ecuador and Bangladesh, the use of cryptocurrencies of any kind is considered illegal.

It is not difficult to understand why many governments are cautious of the use of cryptocurrency. It is always in the policy of the state to protect its people. Considering that nature of cryptocurrency and blockchain, it can be used in the commission of criminal acts like money laundering. Another reason is that cryptocurrency can be considered as a competitor of legal tender currency such as the US dollar. If the demand for cryptocurrency increase and the demand for US dollar (or any other currency of legal tender) decreases, there is a good reason to believe that the value of the legal tender concerned would drop, and this can adversely affect the economy of a state.

The good news is that more and more individuals, businesses, and governments are being open to the use of cryptocurrency. In fact, if you examine the present trend, you will easily see that cryptocurrency is getting more acceptable medium and substitute for money.

Other kinds of cryptocurrencies

There are more than 900 cryptocurrencies that have been made, and more are still being developed. Among all these cryptocurrencies, Bitcoin remains the number one cryptocurrency. However, there are other cryptocurrencies that are doing well in the market. Let us examine these other notable cryptocurrencies:

Ethereum

Ethereum logo

Ethereum is currently the second most popular cryptocurrency next to bitcoin. However, unlike bitcoin that functions merely as a cryptocurrency, Ethereum also functions as a decentralized blockchain and application platform. It features the effective use of smart contract and DApps, among others. It can run applications and services on the blockchain. Because of its interesting features, it has drawn lots of attention and interest in the cryptocurrency community.

Ripple

Ripple logo

Ripple is a form of cross-border payment platform, especially made for financial institutions, such as digital exchanges, financial payment providers, and banks. Unlike most cryptocurrencies that seem to set a different direction and take the place of banks, ripple supports banks, as well as other similar institutions. Although its price is far from that of bitcoin or Ethereum, it has shown substantial growth in terms of its percentage in 2017. Based on its current trend, there is a rising demand for it as it effectively minimizes the cost of international money transfer.

Litecoin

Litecoin logo

Litecoin is not a new coin in the cryptocurrency industry. It was born when people realized that bitcoin had some shortcomings of its own. Litecoin can confirm transactions much faster than bitcoin and also offers "scrypts" as proof of its work. It also has a larger supply than bitcoin. Although its price is nothing near to that of bitcoin, it can still be considered a good investment. In fact, its price increased to more than $50 USD in July 2017.

Dash

Dash logo

Dash coin is a form of open-source p2p cryptocurrency. It is also called as "Digital Cash." it is worth noting that unlike other cryptocurrencies, Dash coin is funded by an autonomous organization. Its features are just like those of bitcoin and litecoin. In addition, it also allows instant transactions (InstaSend), as well as private transactions (PrivateSend). If you examine its trend, you will notice a high increase in 2017. Just in July of 2017, its price shot up to more than $300 USD. Many experts believe that the price of Dash will experience more increase in the coming years.

Zcash

Zcash logo

Zcash offers more secure transactions. If you want to make transactions more private, then Zcash is the cryptocurrency for you. It allows transactions to be "shielded." With Zcash, the sender's information as well as that of the receiver's can be protected, including the amount involved in the transaction. When it comes to privacy enhancement, then Zcash is the way to go.

Namecoin

Namecoin logo

What makes Namecoin completely different from other cryptocurrencies is that it is a domain registrar. It is like GoDaddy or NameCheap, but will give you a *.bit* domain. Hence, if you want *abc* as your domain name, you will have a URL of *abc.bit*. However, this domain can only be browsed if you use the Namecoin wallet software. Namecoin is for those who want to have a domain that is not as public the usual. Also, if you want a domain that can be anonymous, then Namecoin can help you do just that.

MATT COHEN

CHAPTER 3
WAYS TO PROFIT

Make money

The blockchain revolution and development of cryptocurrencies have become a subject of interest to investors and traders. Yes, there are ways that you can profit from these developments. Did you know that had you invested even just $1,000 in bitcoin way back in 2010 then you would have been a multimillionaire by now? The good news is that cryptocurrencies these days as powered by blockchain technology remain to be lucrative investments. Here are the ways that you can make a good amount of money:

Investing

Of course, when it comes to making a profit, investing in cryptocurrency should be on the list. Take note that you do not invest in blockchain; rather, you invest in a cryptocurrency that uses the blockchain technology, such as bitcoin. It is also worth noting that just like any other investments, there are also risks involved when you invest in cryptocurrency. There good news is that there are strategic measures or strategies that you can observe in order to increase your chances of making the right investment decisions. This will be discussed in more detail later in the book.

Trading

Trading cryptocurrency can also be a lucrative business. There are many traders who make thousands of dollars in just a few days with some of them earning as high as 1,000% profit return. Trading is just like investing but entails a more active approach. You can easily make multiple trades in a single day with just a few clicks of a mouse.

It is worth noting that the terms *investing* and *trading* can be used synonymously. After all, when you trade cryptocurrency or anything that has value, you also need to invest some money into that venture. And, when you invest in anything, you will soon have to trade it (sell) for profit.

Mining

Mining cryptocurrency, especially bitcoin, easily became very famous. Take note that the blockchain is composed of blocks. Now, for a certain transaction to be recorded on the ledger, the block concerned must be mined. If it is not mined, then it will remain unconfirmed and the transaction will not be completed. This is the job of miners. Miners solve a complex mathematical problem when they mine. They are rewarded a small fee for every block that they successfully mine. A higher hash rates means faster mining speed.

It is worth noting that majority of cryptocurrency users do not engage in mining. Rather, they just purchase cryptocurrency and make an investment. Mining is still possible today. There are three ways to mine cryptocurrency: Hardware mining, software mining, and cloud mining.

- Hardware mining

This means mining using a mining hardware. Take note that when you use a mining hardware, you will use it together with your computer, preferably a desktop computer.

It is also worth noting that even your computer alone can mine cryptocurrency; however, the problem is that a regular computer does not have enough hash rate to mine a good amount of cryptocurrency. You will only end up with more expenses on electricity than the amount of cryptocurrency that you earn, or you might just be able to profit a negligible amount. Hence, people still buy a mining hardware.

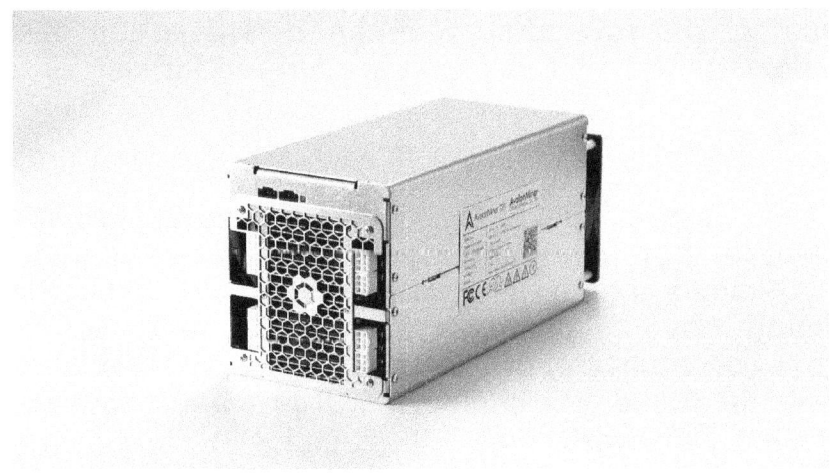

Avalon 721, a Bitcoin miner

The problem with this approach is that a mining hardware that can mine well can be expensive. Also, even with a mining hardware, it can be hard to tell how much you can earn. Another problem with hardware mining is overheating. There are many reports that those who mine using a hardware (and their computer) end up breaking their computers due to overheating issue. This is because mining would take hours on a regular basis just so you can mine a decent amount of cryptocurrency. Hence, hardware mining as an individual may not be a good choice.

- Software mining

If there is hardware mining, then there is also software mining. With software mining, you simply must download a software or just create an account and start mining online. Now this may seem like the best deal; however, the problem with this approach is that you may not be able to earn a good amount of cryptocurrency unless you spend money to upgrade your account. Also, you will have to be online in order to mine cryptocurrency. You can find many mining software that you can download for free online, as well as those that are offered for sale.

- Cloud mining

These days, it seems that cloud mining is the most favored approach to mining. So, how does this work? With cloud mining, a company will mine for you. You simply have to make an investment, and wait for your cryptocurrency to be deposited into your account. Usually, a company will provide a powerful mining hardware that will do all the mining. You simply have to open an account with the company and invest in a miner provided by the company. You will then receive a part from the company's mining profit corresponding to the amount that you have invested. With cloud mining, you no longer have to spend time online. The company will do all the work for you. If you want to get a higher return, then you will have to upgrade your miner.

Although cloud mining appears to be the best approach to mining, it is worth noting that it is not without any issue. Although you will get an expected return, for example, "Invest 1 bitcoin and get 0.01 bitcoin every week," such is only the expected return. Unfortunately, there have been many reports that people who engage in cloud mining get lower than the said expected return. Also, before you engage in cloud mining, be sure to work only with a trusted and reliable mining company. Sadly, there are many scammers online, so be sure to check the latest reviews on a company before you make any deposit.

Is it still a good idea to mine for cryptocurrency? This is a common question asked by those who are starting to learn about cryptocurrency. Now, you may be able to find conflicting views regarding this matter. However, this book suggests that if you are serious about making a significant amount of profit, then you should instead learn how to trade cryptocurrencies. The problem with mining is that it is often outside of your control. You are not assured how much cryptocurrency you can actually mine. If it were that simple then bit-shot investors and traders would have just joined cloud mining companies. However, they know that earning a significant amount and a continuous flow of income would take much more effort.

Gambling

The cryptocurrency revolution has dominated the gambling industry. There are many websites online that offer gambling with bitcoin and other cryptocurrencies. So, why would you like to gamble using cryptocurrency? When you gamble using cryptocurrency, you will have lots of casino choices online. Most cryptocurrency gambling casinos also use a *provably fair* gaming feature. This will allow you to check and verify that the outcome of every round or game is fair and completely random. There are many people who doubt the fairness of online casino games. With the provably fair feature, you can be sure that the casino is not cheating on you.

Still, there are people who do not trust the provably fair feature and would like to have a more realistic gaming experience. The good news is that there are many cryptocurrency casinos that offer live casino gaming. The cards will be dealt in real time by a real and professional casino dealer. How do you know for sure that it is not a pre-recorded video? Well, you can always talk with the beautiful dealer via the chat window while you play. This is like bringing the whole casino into the comfort of your home.

Another benefit of gambling using cryptocurrency instead of using your Visa card is the speed of the transaction. Take note that when you use cryptocurrency, you will be using the blockchain technology. As already explained, transactions over the blockchain are much faster than the typical financial and banking services.

A word of caution: Gambling may not be the best way to make money. In fact, as you may already know, more people lose money in the casino than those who make a profit. The house edge is simply impossible to beat, so you are assured to lose in the long run. Even the genius, Albert Einstein, said that the only way to beat roulette is to steal money from the casino. Of course, this does not literally mean that you should steal money from the casino or anyone. Rather, what it means is that there is simply no way to beat the casino. Therefore, if you ever gamble, do not expect to make money out of it. Gamble for fun and not for profit. If you get lucky, you might be able to end a session with a good profit.

Make your own cryptocurrency

Another way to earn a nice income with cryptocurrency is by making your own cryptocurrency. The truth is that cryptocurrencies are not hard to make. If you have even basic C++ knowledge, then you can easily make your very own cryptocurrency. If people accept and support your creation, then just imagine how much profit you can make.

The real challenge when it comes to making your own cryptocurrency is public acceptance and public use. You need to be able to convince people to accept what you offer, as well as to continuously use it. After all, if there is no demand for your cryptocurrency, then it will not have a value. Hence, many cryptocurrency developers add certain features to their cryptocurrency. For example, the cryptocurrency known as dark coin makes transactions even more private than the ordinary bitcoin transaction over the blockchain. What it does is combine a legitimate transaction with "fake" transactions. Hence, even when people view your transaction over the blockchain, since it will be seen together with other "fake" transactions, it will be almost impossible for them to identify your transaction. Another example is Ethereum which capitalizes on the use of smart contracts. The important thing is to offer value to the market so that people would find it useful.

It is worth noting that offering a cryptocurrency that offers value is only part of the business of creating our own cryptocurrency. The next important thing that you should work on is drawing the interest of the market. After all, even if you have the best cryptocurrency to offer, you cannot expect for it to be successful if the people are not aware that it even exists. A good advice to build a network is to join and participate in online forums ad groups on cryptocurrency.

Gone are the days when you can just come up with any cryptocurrency and expect for it to make a profit on its own. You should expect for more competition these days. You need to come up with something that the market will find useful, be able to promote it effectively, and build a strong network that will support your cryptocurrency.

Creating your own cryptocurrency and making it "sell" in the market would not be easy. In fact, some people suggest that you just wait for a develop to come up with an idea and a cryptocurrency, and if you think that it can be successful, just ride on. This means that you simply invest in it. Hence, the choice whether you should create your own cryptocurrency is a choice that you need to make. If you want it the hard way, then you are free to come up with your own cryptocurrency. If you want to make it simpler, then just wait for a new and lucrative cryptocurrency to be developed and take advantage of it.

Strategies

Whether you want to invest in or trade cryptocurrency, you need to use effective strategies in order to increase your chances of success. Just like any other investment opportunities, there are risks associated with trading or investing. By using the right strategies, you can significantly turn the odds in your favor.

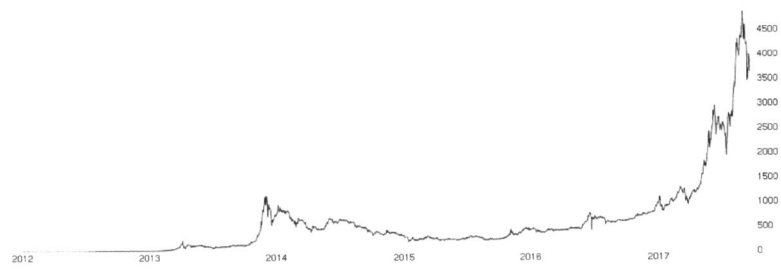

Bitcoin/USD exchange chart (2011 - 2017)

Fundamental analysis

Perhaps considered the most basic of all strategies, fundamental analysis deals with the fundamentals or the basics. For example, if you want to trade bitcoins, then you should study the factors that are affecting its price movement, such as its current market capitalization, its price in comparison with its competitors, as well as the current trend, among others. You should also look at the economy. Do not forget that the prices of cryptocurrencies are highly volatile. But, the more that you know about a particular cryptocurrency, the easier it will be for you to predict its price movement.

Technical analysis

While fundamental analysis heavily relies on analyzing numbers, technical analysis is a more visual approach. With technical analysis, you will be analyzing charts and graphs which reflect the price movements of a cryptocurrency. The theory behind this approach is that all the factors that influence the price of a cryptocurrency have their final effect upon the price. Therefore, just by analyzing how the price of a cryptocurrency moves, you can be able to sum up all the factors and come up with a good investment decision. Since you will be dealing with charts and graphs, expect for this approach to be more visual than fundamental analysis. Most investing or trading platforms will provide you with the tools that you need. If there is none, then there are many sites online that will provide you with the details that you need to analyze the price movements of a particular cryptocurrency.

When you use technical analysis, you should be good at identifying patterns. Hold on — do patterns do exist? The answer is yes. In fact, even a totally random generator creates patterns from time to time. However, it is worth noting that patterns or trends come and go. Therefore, once you see one, be sure to be able to take advantage of it before it changes. Also, avoid the common mistake of seeing a pattern when nothing actually exists.

Buy and hold

The buy and hold strategy is probably the most common strategy that even beginners use. Take note, however, that even though this strategy is used by beginners, it is very effective, especially when you apply it in cryptocurrency. As the name implies, this strategy revolves around buying a particular cryptocurrency. You then simply hold it and wait for its price to increase. Once the price increases, you can then sell it for profit. The key here is to be able to identify the cryptocurrency whose price will most likely increase in the near future.

So, how is it that this simple strategy is effective when you invest in cryptocurrency? The reason is simple: Many of the major cryptocurrencies have increasing prices. There is a good probability that their price will shoot up if you just give them some time. Let us take, for example, the famous cryptocurrency, Bitcoin. Indeed, its price has been continuously fluctuating. There are days when its value shoots up, but there are also days when you see a significant decline in its price. However, if you take a closer look at its long-term price behavior, it is easy to see that its price is on the rise. After all, fluctuations in price is very much normal in cryptocurrency. In fact, even the price of the US dollar and other foreign currencies continuously fluctuate. What is important is its value after a certain lapse of time.

Averaging down

This is an excellent strategy to use, especially if you are looking for an effective way to earn a high amount of profit. The beauty of this strategy is that it allows you to purchase a certain cryptocurrency at a "bargain" price. The best way to explain how this strategy works is by giving an example: Let us say that you want to invest in bitcoin. After studying the cryptocurrency market and think that the price of bitcoin will most likely increase in the future, you then invest in bitcoin by making a buy order. Let us say, for example, that the price of bitcoin is $4,000 USD. So, you purchase some bitcoins at the rate of $4,000. Now, if the price of bitcoin drops, say, down to $3,980, you make another buy order at the said rate of $3,980. If the price drops again, say, to $3,970, you should make another buy order at the said lower rate of $3,970. Now, you might be wondering, how can you profit from this strategy? The key to profit will take place when the price of the cryptocurrency (In this case, bitcoin) increase back to its original amount when you first started to make the investment, or higher. When this happens, then all the buy orders that you have made will experience a profit. Indeed, this is a good and effective strategy.

However, it is worth noting that although this strategy may seem powerful and effective, which it is, you should know that this is considered an aggressive strategy. The reason is that if this strategy does not work, then you will most likely suffer a bad loss. The important part of this strategy is to be able to spot a cryptocurrency whose price will most likely increase after some time. Said time does not have to be tomorrow or within the week. But, it is important that you predict correctly that its price will increase, because it is that increase in price that will earn you a nice profit. Unfortunately, it is not uncommon to find a cryptocurrency whose price shoots down continuously. Sometimes the high volatility of cryptocurrency can be difficult to predict. So, if you ever use this strategy, remember to use it with caution.

Go with the flow

A few months ago, a positive news about bitcoin was published on CNN. As you could expect, the price of bitcoin increased. This is simply how it works. A cryptocurrency that gets a positive publicity or promotion will most likely increase in price.

Conversely, when the news talked about China closing down all of its local bitcoin and cryptocurrency exchanges, the price of bitcoin also dropped. This strategy takes advantage of the "flow." This flow is not hard to read. Simply out, when the news says something positive, then it will most probably result in an increase in price. However, if it is bad news, then expect for the price to decline. The important thing here is to be updated on the news, and to be able to know the news as early as possible. You should also try to understand and predict how cryptocurrency users react. Do not forget that the price of a cryptocurrency primarily depends upon the behavior of the people. A good way to be updated about all these is by following on the news, especially those that are related to cryptocurrency, as well as participating in online groups and forums on the subject.

It is worth noting that merely going with the flow is not always a good strategy. In order to further increase your chances of success, you should also study the cryptocurrency market, so that you will be more able to predict the movements of a particular cryptocurrency.

Value investing

This is an investing strategy that is usually applied when investing in stocks. As the name implies, this is about investing in the value of a cryptocurrency. The key here is to be able to identify a cryptocurrency that has a good value but is currently priced at a lower value than its actual value. The theory behind this strategy is that the market will soon correct itself. When this happens, if the cryptocurrency is currently priced lower than its actual value, then its price will soon increase.

An important part of this strategy is to be able to identify a cryptocurrency that has a good value but is currently priced incorrectly. If you use this approach, you might want to consider new and start-up cryptocurrencies in the market. Start-ups usually have a big room for improvement.

There are many other strategies that you can use. The important thing is not to depend on luck and always apply a strategy to increase your chances of making the right investment or trading decision.

Establish a good network

This is not a strategy per se but can significantly increase your chances of success. It is worth noting that cryptocurrencies, especially new ones, are very sensitive. Their price can fluctuate greatly. It is not uncommon to find the price of a new cryptocurrency to fluctuate even as high as 1,000% in 24 hours. So, what does establishing a good network have to do with this?

The thing is that cryptocurrencies are easier to manipulate than stocks. If you can establish a good network of people who are also active in trading and investing in cryptocurrency, you may, as a group, be able to influence the price movement of a particular cryptocurrency. If you are familiar with the pump and dump scheme in the stock market, then you should be aware that the same scheme applies to cryptocurrency. How does the pump and dump scheme work? Basically, a certain cryptocurrency will be promoted. This way its price will most likely increase. However, what innocent traders do not know is that the promotion is just a hype or a mere manipulation. But, since they will see that the price of a particular cryptocurrency actually increases while it is being "pumped," then the scheme becomes believable. Once the price gets a good increase and more people invest in the cryptocurrency that is being pumped, the people who initiate the scheme will then sell their cryptocurrency for a nice profit. However, the effect of this is that the cryptocurrency will soon drop right after the pump, and all the innocent investors will be in possession of a cryptocurrency whose value is continuously dropping. There are many groups that operate like this in the cryptocurrency environment. Yes, it can be considered fraudulent in a way, but it happens, and it is considered normal. So, either you participate in such group or simply be cautious of being a victim of the pump and dump.

Even if you do not want to participate in any pump and dump scheme, having a good ad active network will still be beneficial for you since it may allow you to gather more useful information. After all, when it comes to investing or trading, having the right information is important to your success.

Buy low, sell high

This is not a strategy per se, but is how you can earn a profit with any trade or investment. This is an old saying: Buy low, sell high. No matter what strategy you use, the objective is to be able to buy low and sell it at a higher price than the price that you bought it. Although this may sound simple, it is much challenging than it seems. When you face the real market and have different cryptocurrencies before you to choose from, it can be hard to identify which cryptocurrencies to buy, as well as those that you should sell. But, if you apply the right strategy and do your research, then your chances of making the right decision will significantly increase. Also, keep in mind not to allow greed to get in the way. Being greedy is an effective way to lose all your profits investment. Be sure to exercise self-control and to always have a plan.

Common mistakes

Now, let us discuss the common mistakes that investors and traders often make. It is important for you to be aware of these pitfalls, in order for you to avoid committing the same mistakes.

Not enough research

This is a very common mistake that you should be cautious of. Many people lose their investment because of insufficient research. It is worth noting that merely surfing the web for an hour is not enough. If you are serious about making a serious flow of income, then you should make sure to do as much research as possible. When it comes to success by investing in cryptocurrency, the amount and quality of information that you have is important. The more that you understand a particular cryptocurrency the easier it will be for you to predict its movement.

Relying on expert advice

If you are a beginner, you may enjoy visiting and listening to the advice of the so-called "experts" online. However, you should know that not all of these "experts" are real experts. In fact, many of them may have more losses than profits. In today's world, it is so easy to promote one's self. Just keep in mind that out of all the people who promote themselves as experts in trading or investing in cryptocurrency, only a few truly understand what they are doing.

Chasing after your losses

Whether investing in or trading cryptocurrency, it is important to keep in mind that you should not chase after your losses. Chasing after one's losses usually occurs right after you experience a bad loss. This is a usual mistake committed by beginners, and even by some advanced traders. The problem is that it is very tempting to chase after one's losses. So, how does a person chase after his losses? Well, normally, when a person chases after his losses, he begins to trade or invest a big amount or percentage of his overall bankroll after he experiences a loss. The aim is to be able to recover the loss and profit even a little. This is not good because the strategy will suddenly turn into an aggressive one, and your current bankroll may not be enough to handle an aggressive approach. For example, many advanced traders only trade 1%-2% of their overall funds per trade. If you suddenly chase after your losses, you may have to spend about 10% or even higher per trade.

It is worth noting that chasing after one's losses does not always mean that you will lose your money. If you get lucky, then you might be able to recover your losses, plus some profit. However, it is worth noting that in the long run, you will most likely have more losses than profits if you continue to chase after your losses.

Money management

Always remember that you should only invest the money that you can afford to lose. Although it is true that investing in cryptocurrency can be a lucrative opportunity, do not forget that it is still an investment; and just like any other investment, it is subject to some risks. Therefore, never use the money that you need to cover for your household expenses, as well as other obligations.

Ideally, you should also have a short-term plan and a long-term plan. Even before you make any kind of investment, you should know your objectives. It is easy to get carried away and be greedy in the middle of an investment, so make sure that you manage your money properly by setting reasonable goals and limitations.

Wrong understanding of volatility

When people talk about cryptocurrencies, they always say that they have a high volatility. But, what does this really mean? *Volatility* refers to change. Hence, when you say that a cryptocurrency has a high volatility, it means that its prices changes significantly within a short period of time. This is true with cryptocurrencies where a price increase or decrease of more than 20% in a day is considered normal.

A common misconception about having a high volatility is that when the price of a cryptocurrency gets a high increase, then it will soon be followed by a significant decrease in price, or vice versa. However, this is not high volatility works. When you say that cryptocurrency has a high volatility, it does not mean that it will balance itself out in the long run. Therefore, what this means is that even if its price experiences a drop, it can still be followed by another decrease in price, and so on. In the same way, an increase in price can continuously be followed by another increase in price. Still, it is also possible that an increase and decrease in price may happen alternately. This is what having a high volatility is all about.

To increase your chances of making the right prediction with respect to its price movement, it is important that you study the different factors that may affect the price of a cryptocurrency. For example, when China decided to close its local bitcoin exchanges, the price of bitcoin experienced a massive drop in price. The good news is that bitcoin was able to recover from it fairly quickly.

MATT COHEN

CHAPTER 4
THE FUTURE OF BLOCKCHAIN

Possible future developments

The blockchain technology is a revolution that has created a strong impact. Still, its technology is considered young with so much room for improvements — which is a good thing. Here are some of the many possibilities of the future of blockchain technology:

There are reasons to believe that central banks will soon be utilizing the use of blockchain. In fact, this is not just limited to the use of blockchain. Many individuals and businesses are also being more open to the use of cryptocurrencies. Hence, both the blockchain technology and cryptocurrencies will be widely used. In fact, banks may soon have an account for cryptocurrency. Today, in some states, you can now withdraw the value of your cryptocurrency into real cash via ATM even without an ATM card.

Stock and trading companies such as the famous NASDAQ may soon switch to a blockchain-enabled platform technology. This will enhance its equity management capabilities, as well as ensure the integrity of all its records.

The blockchain technology can also help in reducing cyber risk. It can offer an identity authentication, which can then be uploaded to a public ledger. The blockchain can also handle the numbering and indexing of records without need of human interference in the process.

Even car rental agencies can benefit from this technology. By harnessing the power of blockchain technology, rentals can be made and authorized as soon as payment is received and upon confirmation of the insurance information. All these can be made possible simply by using blockchain technology with minimal human intervention.

Small businesses can also benefit from blockchain technology by creating a trusted platform for trading. Whether it is for online shopping or just to make a record of the inventory, the blockchain will definitely serve as a helpful tool to implement in a business.

The blockchain technology can also be utilized for crime prevention, as well as to help track down criminals. Criminal information can be sent across all networks in an instant using the blockchain technology. In fact, there is a new blockchain start up today that claims to be able to track down criminals much faster at a low cost. On a negative note, this technology together with the anonymity offered by cryptocurrency can be used in the commission of crimes like money laundering. However, it is worth noting that regulatory measures are being developed in order to prevent this from happening.

If you just consider how much the blockchain technology can develop itself, there are reasons to believe that it will soon be a major part of central banks. In fact, there are those who predict that the blockchain technology can even completely take the place of banks after some more time.

In case of cross-border payments, the cost of UBS's infrastructure can be lowered by billions of dollars every year simply by using the blockchain technology. However, some economists of Deutsche bank consider the blockchain technology as a serious threat on the reasoning that it may lack sufficient IT infrastructure to support this kind of technology in the long run.

Banks may soon realize the benefits of using Ethereum. Ethereum prides itself with its smart contracts, which can be very useful to banks and other financial services.

According to a study, by simply using the blockchain technology, lenders can be able to save billions of dollars every year in settlement.

Retail and manufacturing industries can also enjoy better and more effective supply chain management with the use blockchain technology.

The blockchain technology is not limited to businesses. It can also change how elections are made. In fact, due to its high security, it is an effective technology that can ensure the fairness of all elections.

It is also not hard to believe that cryptocurrencies like bitcoin will soon dominate the financial environment. These cryptocurrencies may soon have the same standing as currencies that are legal tender.

As you can see, the great potential of blockchain technology can bypass today's financial environment completely. However, its technology is still fairly new. More time and education will be needed for the different sectors and industries to realize the benefits that blockchain can offer. Also, as an expected effect of implementing blockchain, it will decrease or totally remove certain jobs, but it will also create new job opportunities.

The future possibilities of the blockchain technology can be said to be infinite. However, it is not yet a completely established technology. There are still many people who are wary of using it. In fact, there are those who do not even trust the blockchain technology and considers it to be just another hype. Hence, there is also the risk that blockchain may just disappear completely. However, if you take a closer look at how things are going for blockchain, as well as the evolution of cryptocurrency, it will not be hard to tell that it has a bright future that is waiting for it.

How blockchain can affect financial services and other employment

Based on the current trend and development of the blockchain technology, many are saying that it will soon take the place of many financial services and other employment. Just now, it is already becoming a better substitute for banks and other third-party financial services like PayPal. Studies also show that the blockchain can soon take the place of accountants, as well as those that are engaged in the keeping and updating of records.

It is now considered a certainty that blockchain will have an impact upon those that engage in financial services. Blockchain is an effective way to cut down the cost and simplify the financial process. Not only that, blockchain also offers more transparency and higher security. These are the main reasons why so many people today are switching to and supporting the blockchain technology.

Although all these seem promising as much as blockchain is concerned, there are still those who think that there would be more disadvantages than advantages when switching to blockchain. Industries that are related to or deal with banking, payments, security, and other financial services, will definitely experience the impact of blockchain in their industry. Chances are that such companies will soon lose value proposition and a decline in sustainable jobs may soon be expected. The introduction of the blockchain technology to business, particularly the financial industry can be likened to the introduction of robotics in the manufacturing industry, which caused some modifications in the way people do their job and also caused in the decline of job opportunities. However, it is also expected that the blockchain technology will soon create new job positions and opportunities, especially related to computers and programming.

Although blockchain may take the place of other employment positions, it seems still unlikely that it will completely remove the need of human intervention or assistance. There is no technology as yet that can guarantee such quality as that of a professional human. However, the blockchain technology is expected to develop even further. With its continuous evolution, less and less human intervention can be expected. In fact, there is now an idea where humans will no longer have to deal with machine. Rather, everything will turn into robotics. Robots will deal with robots with no or minimum human intervention. Whether this is good or not, only the future will know. For now, it can be said that the present time together will blockchain technology is gradually heading towards such future.

The future of money

Money has a long history. However, it seems that money has already met its future: cryptocurrency. In fact, cryptocurrency was just an idea in the past and was even referred to as the future of money. Today, that future which was once only an idea is now a reality. Cryptocurrencies, especially Bitcoin, are so popular and more people are learning about them. As you can notice, the evolution of the Internet paved a way for e-commerce and online businesses to bloom. When it comes to making transactions online, banks may no longer be the best medium that can assist you online. If you make online transactions, then it is more fitting to use online money. And, of course, this is what cryptocurrencies are all about. It is also hard to steal cryptocurrencies because they do not have any physical manifestation. Even banks cannot take them away from you. By using cryptocurrency and the power of blockchain, you get to be more in control of your money.

Today, money can be easily and quickly transferred with just a few clicks of a mouse. Although people can stick to banks and other financial services, it is not hard to realize that when it comes to doing online transactions, cryptocurrencies offer much more convenience, benefits, and ease of use.

Now and then

Today, the blockchain technology and cryptocurrencies can still be considered to be young in their development stage. Still, even as early as now, their impact upon the world, particularly on financial services, can already be seen. More people should also be educated about them. For such technology to work, the people must be educated about it, so that they will accept this new technology and make use of it. Fortunately, the blockchain and cryptocurrency technology are booming that so many people are getting interested in learning about them. In fact, there are many investors and traders who start working on cryptocurrencies.

When talking about blockchain, it will normally be associated with cryptocurrency, for obvious reasons. Today, it is now possible to send and receive cryptocurrencies with just a few clicks of a mouse. In some states, you can also use cryptocurrency to pay for your household bills (water, electricity, etc.). It can also be used to book for a hotel room or even to pay for your air fare for travel, and so much more. Of course, the backbone of all these technological developments is the blockchain technology.

As the blockchain technology continues to improve, more opportunities will open for its use and application. Years from now, blockchain will most probably be the leading structure not only in terms of financial services but also with respect to its other relevant applications like in business, record-keeping, and others.

The future remains a mystery for blockchain. However, by simply examining the past and present trend, you can observe that the blockchain technology is on the rise. It is, indeed, the technology of the future, and that future has arrived.

CONCLUSION

Thanks for making it through to the end of this book. I hope it was informative and able to provide you with all of the tools you need to achieve your goals whatever they may be.

The next step is to apply everything that you have learned. By now you should already have a good foundation and understanding of what the blockchain technology is all about, as well as how it works with cryptocurrencies. There are many reasons why people are learning to use blockchain. Indeed, there are many benefits that you can get from it. And, by learning about blockchain, you can also make a way to earn a profit by investing in or trading cryptocurrencies.

The blockchain technology is not really difficult to understand. In fact, it works quite simply. The important thing for this technology to last is continued public acceptance and use. Since the blockchain technology is drawing lots of attention these days and is continuously being developed, there is a possibility that it will soon reach its highest potential and people would welcome and accept it.

The blockchain technology is still a fairly new technology. It will still undergo lots of changes and developments. Also, many people still need to be educated, so that they will learn to appreciate just how this technology can help them.

Since blockchain is the technology of the future, investing in it today might just be the best investment that you can ever make. Perhaps an easy way to support the blockchain technology is simply to make use of cryptocurrencies like bitcoin. Although this technology may have many wonderful things to offer, it needs the acknowledgment and acceptance of the people. The best way to show support is to make use of it; otherwise, it may start to lose its value.

It is worth noting that despite the many changes that blockchain technology has already done, there are still many developments that we can expect from it in the future. Since the blockchain technology is continuously being developed, it is your job to be updated on the latest news regarding its progress. Now that you understand what blockchain really is, then it is time for you to take advantage of it.

Finally, if you found this book useful in anyway, a review on Amazon is always appreciated!

OTHER BOOKS BY MATT COHEN

Bitcoin: Complete Guide to Mastering Bitcoin Mining, Trading, and Investing

Discover how YOU can make money with Bitcoin

Back in 2010 1 Bitcoin was valued $0.003. Since then its value has been radically increasing. In 2011 Bitcoin took parity with US Dollar, in 2013 it was worth 266$ (an astonishing increase of 26500%). 4 years later 1 Bitcoin was valued roughly 1000$. Because of this insane growth, Bitcoin has been defined as the new gold rush. Making money mining, trading or investing in Bitcoin is completely possible. You're missing a lot of opportunities if you still haven't jump on board, because overall Bitcoin value keeps increasing.

"As of October 2017 1 BITCOIN is valued $4.165".

Bitcoin is different from all the other currencies because no one can control it. Bitcoins are a digital currency exchanged between users through the net, they aren't printed by a central bank and can't be devalued. Thanks to its decentralized nature Bitcoin provides a lot of opportunity for people to profit. However, due to its seemingly complex and technical nature Bitcoin may seem difficult to understand for non-technical users.

Imagine if you could discover the exact tools savvy investors use to make a lot of money trading, mining and investing in Bitcoins.

In this book you'll find everything you need to know about the Bitcoin world and the blockchain technology. You'll discover all the websites and softwares that will give you the ability to earn money trading and investing in bitcoins, and all the tools and platforms you can use to mine bitcoins for a profit. This is an in-depth guide on cryptocurrency and bitcoin, but you'll be easily able to understand it even if you're a non-technical user.

What you'll discover:
- What Is a Bitcoin And How Does It Work
- Everything You Need To Start Mining Bitcoin For Profit
- How To Make Money Quickly Using Bitcoin Mining Platforms
- How To Avoid Losing Money With The Mining Profitability Calculator (100% Risk-Free)
- Trusted Platforms To Start Trading Bitcoin For Profit
- What Drives Bitcoin Price, And How To Take Advantage Of It
- A Scam Test To Discover If A Bitcoin Service Isn't

Legitimate Before Losing Money
- The Best Bitcoin Wallets For Computers And Smartphones
- 10 Important Rules To Keep Your Bitcoins Safe
- And Much, Much More

Don't miss the Bitcoin opportunity!

"Bitcoin" by Matt Cohen is available at Amazon.

www.ingramcontent.com/pod-product-compliance
Lightning Source LLC
Chambersburg PA
CBHW070318230526
45470CB00002B/935